THE GOSPEL OF TECHNOLOGY

Abhijit Naskar is the twenty-first century mind of science, whose seminal philosophical touch has enabled modern Neuroscience to effectively engage in the human society towards diminishing the ever-growing conflicts among religions. As an untiring advocate of global harmony and peace, he became a beloved best-selling author all over the world with his very first book "The Art of Neuroscience in Everything". With various of his pioneering ventures into the Neuropsychology of religious sentiments, he has hugely contributed in the eradication of religious differences in our world, for which he is popularly hailed as a humanitarian neuroscientist, who takes the human civilization in the path of sweet general harmony.

THE
GOSPEL
OF
TECHNOLOGY

ABHIJIT NASKAR

The Gospel of Technology

An Amazon Publishing Company, 1st Edition, 2020

Printed in the United States of America

ISBN: 9781660457854

Also by Abhijit Naskar

The Art of Neuroscience in Everything
Your Own Neuron: A Tour of Your Psychic Brain
The God Parasite: Revelation of Neuroscience
The Spirituality Engine
Love Sutra: The Neuroscientific Manual of Love
Homo: A Brief History of Consciousness
Neurosutra: The Abhijit Naskar Collection
Autobiography of God: Biopsy of A Cognitive Reality
Biopsy of Religions: Neuroanalysis towards Universal
Tolerance
Prescription: Treating India's Soul
What is Mind?
In Search of Divinity: Journey to The Kingdom of Conscience
Love, God & Neurons: Memoir of a scientist who found
himself by getting lost
The Islamophobic Civilization: Voyage of Acceptance
Neurons of Jesus: Mind of A Teacher, Spouse & Thinker
Neurons, Oxygen & Nanak
The Education Decree
Principia Humanitas
The Krishna Cancer
Rowdy Buddha: The First Sapiens
We Are All Black: A Treatise on Racism
The Bengal Tigress: A Treatise on Gender Equality
Either Civilized or Phobic: A Treatise on Homosexuality
Wise Mating: A Treatise on Monogamy
Illusion of Religion: A Treatise on Religious
Fundamentalism
The Film Testament
Human Making is Our Mission: A Treatise on Parenting
I Am The Thread: My Mission
7 Billion Gods: Humans Above All
Lord is My Sheep: Gospel of Human
Morality Absolute
A Push in Perception
Let The Poor Be Your God
Conscience over Nonsense
Saint of The Sapiens
Time to Save Medicine
Fabric of Humanity

Build Bridges not Walls: In the name of Americana
The Constitution of The United Peoples of Earth
Lives to Serve Before I Sleep
When Humans Unite: Making A World Without Borders
All For Acceptance
Monk Meets World
Mission Reality
Citizens of Peace: Beyond The Savagery of Sovereignty
Operation Justice
See No Gender

To
Nikola Tesla

CONTENTS

Smartness without
Wisdom is Stupidity

What do I know? What do you know? And what do you not know? What do I not know? These are the questions that you should be asking if you want to understand the difference between knowledge and ignorance. More and more I am beginning to see in the society, the illusion of knowledge. And this illusion is not about ignorance. Ignorance is everywhere - it's in every single person - by which I literally mean every single person, including myself.

Every person has some sort of ignorance about something. Nobody can know about everything - no one person can see the whole picture - it is a biological impossibility - hence, it is an existential impossibility. But that is not the problem - ignorance is not the problem. Ignorance is rather healthy. What's not healthy is illusion of knowledge.

Illusion of knowledge is lethal - it's dangerous, because it makes people believe that their belief is the only truth - that their belief is a fact - and that is devastating because, it not only keeps them away from the real understanding of a phenomenon, but also it creates a barrier between them and the people who actually, genuinely want to understand.

What is wrong in accepting that you do not know! There is nothing wrong in accepting that you do not know, in fact, knowledge begins with the acceptance of ignorance. If you do not even accept that you do not know, then how can you even actually begin to know! To even begin to understand something - to even begin to realize something - to learn about something you have to first know what you do not know.

For example, there are a lot of things I do not know, but the one thing I do know is that there are a lot of things I do not know. If you keep on believing and deluding yourself that you know something based on your faith, your tradition, your culture, your comfort level, your mystical ideals, then no knowledge will ever manifest in your mind.

Let me elaborate. There was a time when people believed that the light that we see in the day sky comes from a deity called "Ra" – the Sun God. But with the arrival of evidence – with the arrival of facts, we got rid of such imaginative ideas – ideas that our ancestors came up with due to lack of evidence – due to lack of understanding. They hailed all nature to be possessed by some form of supernatural force.

They feared every single natural manifestation of power, like thunderstorms, droughts, rain, floods, earthquakes, landslides, volcanoes, fire, heat, and cold etc. To avoid intellectual effort they had to incorporate supernatural explanations to those phenomena. They basically suspected that all those natural events were the gods' way of showing that they were angry with our ancestors. Naturally, our primitive ancestors felt the urge to appease that anger by worshipping nature.

They started to worship all the elements of Mother Nature like stones, hills, trees, lakes, animals and many more as some deity or supernatural force. They believed that souls or spirits exist, not only in humans, but also in inanimate objects such as plants, rocks, mountains, rivers and other entities of the natural environment.

But we have come a long way since then. Now people in general no longer hold such supernatural beliefs about the elements of nature at least. Most of the human population has become mature enough in their psyche to accept the basic facts of the world we live in. Most people now know that the sun is simply a star in the sky giving light and not some luminous deity riding his chariot. Likewise, unlike our ancestors, today's humanity now accepts the fact that the earth is not the center of the universe.

The point is, if we are to move forward in the path of understanding – in the path of knowledge – in the path of truth – we must accept certain facts as they come to light. We cannot simply ignore the facts, just because they are not compatible with our beliefs – the beliefs that we are used to – just because they are not compatible with the traditions that we have been following for centuries or millennia.

So, have the courage - have the decency - have the humility to accept your ignorance. In these virtues lies the seed of wisdom. And wisdom is the only phenomenon that can ensure a healthy progressive future of a species. It's not enough to be the smartest species on earth, we must put that smartness to good use without ruining our mental as well as physical health. Smartness without wisdom is stupidity. Sometimes the smartest people on earth act like the stupidest people on earth. Smartness is not the measure of progress, it is only an ingredient in progress, which requires the guidance of wisdom to be utilized in the most prosperous manner.

There's Reason
to Be Worried

Only with wisdom can you perceive the actual implications of technology in human life and society, and when you do, you'll be horrified to your bones, as much as I am at the sight of the future that is slowly creeping into the life of our children. I am worried – terribly worried – for our kids and their kids – for the citizens of tomorrow – and this is no everyday worry, for everyday worries come and go, but this worry is not going to fade away. I am worried for the sanity of our kids and all the kids yet to come.

We have arrived at a point of time where the way we raise our kids is going to draw the line between sanity and insanity – it's going to draw the line between the will to live and the urge to give up. Never in history, was the situation as severe as it is now. And if you genuinely want your kids to have a healthy and happy life, then you no longer have the luxury to be callous about their daily habits.

Here I am not addressing your capacity for raising kids, for that's an instinctual response which comes naturally to all parents, but what I am pointing out is that, even that age-old parental instinct of raising children is not going to be enough in ensuring that the kids grow up to be mentally stable members of a healthy society. Mark this, if you do not get serious right now, then the future that awaits your kids will be that of insanity, misery and death – not metaphorically, but quite literally.

Technology – that's what revolutionized this planet beyond human imagination when it came to existence – and now in its newly acquired digital form, it has begun to revolutionize our society once again, except this time the repercussions are turning out to be a thousand times greater than all of the previous technological revolutions combined.

Selfies have begun to replace memories – likes and comments have begun to replace lasting conversations – illusive friends and followers lists have begun to replace real reliable friendship. And this is nothing to be taken for granted, for the digital innovation that set out to connect people, has slowly started to tear those people apart both from within and without.

Reliability has become scarce – commitment has become scarce – attachment has become scarce. The very socio-psychological mechanisms that sustain the stability and wellness of a society are beginning to collapse, and when they do, the very fabric of societal stability and sanity will get ripped apart, which I am afraid is no longer a possibility.

This has already begun to happen and the situation will only get worse, creating a society full of sociopaths, psychopaths and basically unstable, depressed and superficial human beings with no strength of character and conscience, and no sense of patience and sanity whatsoever. They will crave for appraisal – they will crave for attention – they will crave for flattery – they will crave for perfection. Everything about them will be artificial and superficial. And no matter how much they pretend to present their life as perfect, inside they will be dying every single second of their existence.

Now the question is, what are we going to do about it? Are we going to do anything at all? Are you going to do anything at all? Are you? I am asking again and again, because upon this question depends the very stability and sanity of our children and grandchildren. If you can perceive the impending doom, then we can move to actions.

The best way to teach the children a habit is to adopt it ourselves. So, the first step to raise a society that will know the distinction between healthy use of technology and harmful use of technology, is to practice that distinction religiously in our own lives. This means that you must right this very moment start modulating your use of devices, by turning off all notifications except the most important ones.

You do not actually need to delete your social media accounts, but what you must do is – and I mean must, not should, because if I ask you, do you want to protect your child from committing suicide, then you would probably say, you must, not should – so, what you must do is, check your social media only once or twice a day – at most three times, but not more. And this applies to all the responsible adults everywhere, whether you are at home, at work or in transit. Because, if you can't be the role model for the children of this world, not just your own children, then you have no right to blame those kids for their behavior.

So, renounce the 24/7 smartphone scrolling behavior, if you actually care for the future of your kids – for the future of this world. Then comes giving a little nudge to your kids when you see them being consumed by their devices. You may say, they won't listen. Actually, they do not listen because you do not give them enough time from an early age. Spend time with them – watch a movie with them – go for an outing with them – do something with them whenever you have time. Set the standards of healthy living in front of the children, by being an embodiment of healthy living yourself, then and then only will there be hope for the kids to turn into responsible, stable, patient and socially functional human beings.

Character of Technology Comes From its Creator

If humankind is the greatest invention of mother nature, then technology is the greatest invention of humankind. Mother Nature gave us (not to be taken literally, because I am using the term "mother nature" to refer to the collective processes taking place in nature) the power of thought and conscience to decide for ourselves what's right, what's wrong - what's good, what's evil. Now some of us are trying to do the same with technology, and to some very basic non-conscious extent we have succeeded to do so. But we are yet to endow technology with actual awareness, which will be the most titanic task ever achieved, if we ever in a very very distant future be able to do so.

If a machine ever gains awareness, it will be not due to our careful programming, but due to an unforeseeable anomaly. All great achievements are born of anomalies. To achieve the unachieved, one has to do the undone, which in most cases is seen by the society as an anomaly. Yet the bridge of progress is founded solely on the pillars of these anomalous achievements. Hence, without anomaly, progress is non-existent - without the misfit visionaries, progress is non-existent.

Inside the biological realm of the cells, this process of anomalous activity is called mutation. And while in some cases, mutation can lead to certain genetic disorders, it is the major source of variation in the natural world, as well as the very ingredient of evolution. It is the only process through which "new" traits manifest in a species. Likewise, mutation of thought opens up new frontiers of progress.

No invention has ever been made which has not been used for both good and evil purposes. And here, I beg you not to associate the term evil with something mystical or supernatural, rather "evil" is any simple human deed that makes a detrimental effect on the human society, either directly, such as through bigotry, racism and phobias, or indirectly, such as through climate change denial. Now, the question is, can we ever build a society, where no power will be used for any kind of evil purposes?

And the answer is, power has no conscience of its own - power is only a lifeless, motionless potential, which comes to life, the moment it gains momentum by the force of human will. If that will is driven by a humane sense of conscience, then it'll utilize the power for not just the good of the self but more importantly for the good of the society, whereas, if that will is driven the force of bigotry, then it is very much likely that it'll utilize the power in inhuman ways, without even being aware of it.

So long as humankind lives as an organic species, there will be both good and bad. However, to make sure that the bad doesn't overwhelm the healthy functioning of our society, we must, not should, but must, do our individual bit to contribute to the collective good of the humankind. The goodness of humankind is predicated upon the goodness of the individual. Without the goodness of the individual, there is no goodness of the humankind.

Which means, whether a power does good to the society or not, depends upon the action of the individual. With each drop of good from the veins of each individual, will the ocean of serenity, peace and acceptance be born. The world consists of nations – a nation consists of people - a people consists of individuals - an individual consists of psychological elements, collectively called "the mind" - and a mind is a product of a hundred billion nerve cells working relentlessly in proper harmony. Thus, a little change in the neural network inside one human brain, has the potential to essentially influence a whole nation, and even a whole world.

Algorithms are Aid
not Substitute

The purpose of algorithms is to expand our capacities, not to substitute us humans altogether. And this applies to every single technological marvel that we have been encountering in the recent times, such as social media, virtual reality, artificial intelligence, blockchain technology and so on.

Let's take blockchain for example, since I have already gone into the matter of artificial intelligence in one of my previous works, entitled "Mission Reality". Blockchain technology can be a supplement to the traditional human-based financial system, but not a substitute. Because by doing so, we would literally be handing over all our economic and financial matters of the society to computer algorithms. It's a complicated matter, so let's move very slowly. Don't rush to make conclusions, because if you do, then there is no use of our investigation.

Some argue that computers will deal with our financial matters better than the humans. And indeed - in an ideal, errorless world, that would definitely be the case, but any student of basic computer sciences can tell you that no computer is immune to bugs, that is, algorithmic anomaly, be it humanly created or spontaneously generated. And all it takes is one bug to cause a global collapse of economy of catastrophic proportions.

In a human-based, that is, institution-based financial system, the very job of experts and professionals is to avoid such collapse, or to attempt to fix such collapse if and when it happens. But in a decentralized system, there is no expert, no professional, no guiding angel that you can rely on, either for your personal financial issues, or in case of a global financial crisis. Now let's understand the matter of decentralization a bit deeply.

For example, even the internet is not decentralized. It is run by institutions such as google, twitter, facebook and so on. The sole purpose of these companies, or at least most of them (as facebook consistently keeps telling people, even hate speech and fake news fall under the protection of free speech, so fact checking does not apply to any of the content on their platform), is to provide as much helpful information as possible while cancelling out as much harmful and fake content as possible.

And just imagine, even in the hands of institutions, the internet is not yet a healthy sphere for information - it's getting increasingly filled with fake news, hate speech, abusive trolls and so on - so what would happen if we take away the guiding hands of those institutions altogether! It would be an absolute chaos. And the same is true for a financial system, and in fact any other system of the society.

So in short, blockchain itself is not dangerous, but if we start using decentralized blockchain as a complete substitute for our traditional transaction methods, then I am afraid, it would destroy the very human foundation of our financial system. We are not a mechanical species, we are a living breathing organic species, which means, we are always making mistakes - and we keep growing, because we can learn from our mistakes - but if we think we could just develop a few algorithms and hand all the financial matters of our society over to them, then such is not a healthy futuristic dream, rather it's a nightmare.

We must never even dream of leaving important functionings of our society on computer algorithms – fully that is. We can use algorithms as an aid to the systems of our society, like pilots use autopilot, but we must never let them run our society completely on their own - the day we do, will be the day we fall.

For example, some magnificent algorithms can now predict the credit-worthiness of someone wanting a short-term loan. And through a mobile application that runs on those algorithms, a user can get a loan from the bank in less than ten seconds after inputting the data. In these few seconds the algorithm assesses thousands of personal features from all your data. The algorithm can dig up information that can never be apparent to a human loan officer. This is only one among the millions of ways that algorithms do and can help humanity.

To predict the weather today's experts use computer models that work on the very foundation of artificial intelligence. By focusing on improving the machine learning algorithms of the artificial intelligence used in weather predictions, we could predict forthcoming storms and other catastrophic weather events, much more accurately and far earlier - this will naturally help save many more lives than we can today. Also, every piece of digital technology that's being used today in our healthcare system worldwide, works on the basis of some form of machine learning program or artificial intelligence. And improving them would naturally mean improving the healthcare system.

In all these distinct fields, it's the humans who use artificial intelligence algorithms as tools to serve humanity, but the accountability always lies on the humans, which makes the algorithms trustworthy, because we know that if something goes wrong there are people we can rely on for answers and solution. However, in decentralization, this very fundamental societal fabric of reliance and trust is non-existent – and the advocates of such a system actually promote this feature as some sort of advanced quality of a superior species.

But here is the thing. Leaving society to algorithms will be like leaving healthcare to stethoscopes. Technology is a huge part of healthcare, but it's the doctors and nurses who use those technologies, not the other way around. So, even if we do use blockchain technology, or in fact any such technology, in our society, we must use it in a centralized manner, not in a decentralized manner.

With centralization comes accountability, whereas with decentralization comes chaos. Centralized blockchain can be a great boon to the society, especially in the developing parts of the world, whereas decentralized blockchain will only cause chaos and destruction.

With decentralized blockchain technology, the power goes to the individual, and so does the responsibility, which means that liability for any kind of loss in such would lies on no one else but the individual user of that system. Complete freedom from institutions means complete responsibility on the self. So, though decentralization sounds like a great thing, its actual functionality relies on the absolute, uncompromisable, unshakable self-reliance of the society - a society that requires no intervention from any institution whatsoever.

Now, the question is, does this sound sensible enough?

Also, the advocates of decentralized blockchain technology also proclaim it to be invincible, which is nothing but a childish stupidity. There are countless ways for your personal blockchain gateway data to be stolen. No technology that's connected to the internet is unhackable - anybody who thinks it is, is either lying to promote their bitcoin mining career or has no practical understanding of how computers work.

Cryptocurrency itself has no value of its own, unlike other tangible assets such as gold or real estate or even a simple service such as netflix or spotify. Currency is like God, it exists as long as people believe in it. So, decentralized cryptocurrency is only valid as long as a lot of people start using it as an actual means of transactions. The so-called miners who are just regular people maintaining the basic infrastructure of computers that carry out the fundamental confirmation processes of transactions called "Proof-of-Work" in a public distributed ledger called the blockchain, get rewarded in bitcoins, which can only be used if actual merchants start accepting them as a valid means of payment, which a few merchants are doing already despite the ridiculously volatile nature of decentralized cryptocurrency.

So, of course, the miners would advocate for decentralized cryptocurrency, but if you ask them, *"will you personally help out the people find their lost cryptocurrency if their device or their private cryptocurrency key is hacked or lost"* - all their intellectualism concerning a decentralized financial system will fall apart.

Just imagine, all the savings that person has acquired by working day in day out, is lost just in a blink of an eye, and he or she has literally no one to turn to, because decentralized cryptocurrency literally means that you cannot call anyone for help. That's where the role of the banks comes in.

The purpose of a centralized financial system or any other system, is not to exploit people, but to ensure stability in the society. In short, incorporating cryptocurrency in the traditional centralized financial system not only speeds up transactions exponentially, but also it makes the system more user-friendly, whereas in a decentralized system cryptocurrency will only breed insecurity and chaos, due to the utter absence of liability. In all social systems there are always some people who abuse their power, but still, a flawed human-based organic system is a million times better than an apparently flawless, completely autonomous mechanical algorithm.

Those who are trying to push decentralized cryptocurrency as a payment solution for the unbanked population of the developing countries, have no actual clue to the physical as well as psychological living conditions of those people. These so-called advocates of decentralized blockchain technology are just pompous, arrogant and sophisticated intellectuals living in glass castles far away from the grassroots, who think of technology to be the ultimate solution to all the problems of this world without taking any tangible responsibility for the troubles of the people. Technology is power. And any form of power has the potential to corrupt its possessor. So, ultimately it all comes down to individual responsibility.

Think of facebook for example. No matter how direct and real implications the content on this platform have on the lives of the people around the world, it still hasn't gained the mental maturity to take responsibility for those implications. This could perhaps make sense if it was a decentralized platform run completely by computers with no humans involved, but it's not. It is a platform run by a person who makes money through user engagement without giving any practical thought to user health and their right to fact-checked information.

Facebook keeps boasting that it won't take down any content even if they are lies, because that violates their, or perhaps I should just say Mark's principle on free speech. If we take this argument to be a functional argument in civilized society, then we should not punish pedophilia either, because it violates the pedophile's freedom of expression - the same goes for polygamy - the same goes for racism - the same goes for homophobia.

This is what happens when a person naively presumes that developing an algorithm to connect people will only have beneficial impact on the society. The problem is not Mark Zuckerberg's inability to foresee the adverse effects of his platform - the real problem is his stubborn indifference to even the current effects, in the name of defending free speech. I am afraid this only makes him sound like a brainless bot with no conscience or sense of responsibility, despite all his coding capacity.

There is no question that social media and internet all together have enabled the human species to take a vast leap in the path of advancement. But the point is, in the process, it has also started to the break the very soul of the human species. Now, here I am not saying that it would have been better if we didn't invent social media or internet all together, but the point I am making is, technologically humanity has exceeded the limits of its own psychological capacity.

We have the social media and internet all right, and they can indeed become great tools of progress, but the problem is, we are not psychologically capable of utilizing such vast power without fundamentally ruining our internal order and wellbeing. To solve the problems created by social media platforms, many politicians are now giving the call to break up big tech. Empowered by their own limited understanding of the matter and blinded by their own biases, their brain has made them believe that impeding the growth of big tech companies will magically give power back to the people. Here they act just like another kind of anti-intellectuals, who can't even perceive the real problem, so they think of breaking up the companies as the ultimate solution.

Therefore, I am not advocating for breaking up big tech and handing over its power to the government, for it would only replace one authority with another. Handing over the authority of facebook to any one institution or person would automatically make that platform biased towards the interest of that institution or person, just like it is now.

So, breaking up big tech is not the solution, nor is letting things go on the way they are going. The only solution here is responsibility, that is accountability. We can't hold an algorithm responsible, for an algorithm has no conscience of its own, but we must hold the person, people or institution in control of that algorithm accountable, if we are to give a safe, hate-free and above all humane society to our children. And remember, do not think of these statements of mine to be my professional statements, for it's not mere professional, it's personal - it's personal to me - it's personal to you - and it's personal to every single living human who is concerned for the future of their children.

My entire body of work is personal - there is nothing professional about it - because being professional means abiding by a certain set of principles, often compromising basic humanity, which I am afraid is no sign of a conscientious species. Professionalism is death, for it's driven by obedience, whereas a true sense of responsibility automatically makes you act. Responsibility brings action and action brings excellence, which brings more effective action.

Technology won't save this world - reason won't save this world - faith won't save this world – only responsibility will. If you are responsible above all forms of loyalty and attachment to external forces and authorities, then there takes place a psychological inpouring of clarity - a clarity in which you can hail the right place and effective implications of every form of potential - be it technology, reason, faith or anything else.

Every force has its place, but if you are obsessively attached to any one force, your mind automatically becomes cognitively biased towards that force and blind to even the greatest benefits of other forces. So, you must be very cautious about placing your loyalty on any external force. When you are too sure about your beliefs on external forces, your mind automatically turns you blind towards not just the shortcomings of your beliefs, but to obvious facts of the world as well.

Even with the mammoth amount of more than 100 trillion synapses in your brain, you only have access to a tiny sliver of reality of the world. On top of that, you are in all circumstances inclined to your own beliefs in your understanding of the universe. To test this inclination, some of scientists have devised a beautiful study using syllogisms. But before I tell you more about the study, let me tell you a bit about what a syllogism is.

A syllogism is a kind of logical argument that applies deductive reasoning to arrive at a conclusion based on two or more propositions that are asserted or assumed to be true. Aristotle defined it as a form of conclusion decided from the combination of a general statement (the major premise) and a specific statement (the minor premise). The simplest example of syllogism is this:

All men are mortal (major premise). Socrates is a man (minor premise). Therefore, you can validly conclude that Socrates is mortal.

Now let's get back to the study I was talking about. Scientists used various proreligious and antireligious syllogisms to analyze how believers and non-believers think when it comes to making logical decisions. The following syllogisms were part of their study.

Proreligious Syllogism: If to succeed in life you have to be Christian, and if a person named Thomas wants to succeed in life, then Thomas should become a Christian.

Antireligious Syllogism: If being religious is found to be bad for people who have depression, and if you suffer from depression, then you should try to be less religious.

Participants were asked to evaluate whether the syllogisms were internally logical or not. The results were absolutely enthralling. The religious people did better on the proreligious questions, and the nonreligious people did better on the antireligious questions. The results imply that both groups make logical mistakes, but they make them in the direction of their beliefs.

So, ultimately the point is, it is not easy being the most advanced species on planet earth. It requires various elements of beliefs, ideas and emotions in order to sustain our sense of being human throughout the lifetime. Each brain builds various unique cognitive mechanisms in order to ensure the survival of the self on the planet.

As you grow up and go through various events of life, you learn new ideas and behaviors, meet new people, and continue to develop as a person. Throughout the lifetime, your brain maintains your sense of self-identity while processing and adapting to all the changes in your life.

Your biology has one simple purpose in life, i.e. to survive. And your bran facilitates this purpose through its function of self-maintenance. This function consists of everything that your brain does to ensure your survival. It includes your usual everyday activities, such as eating, drinking and mating, as well as your innate instinct of defying all ideas that contradict your belief system. All the structures and functions of your brain ultimately enable you to navigate the complex and occasionally threatening physical world in which you live.

But the point here is that, all of these self-maintenance mechanisms were evolved in the human anatomy to ensure our survival in the wild, but we no longer live in such an environment that demands a creature to be ferocious in order to live. So, it is imperative that we make our biology, or to be more specific our mind, shift its focus from a fierce individualistic survival to a healthy collective global existence. But this can't happen overnight and more importantly this can't happen by force.

To shift the instinctive focus of your mind from self-preservation to what's right and healthy for all humankind, you must make the conscious and conscientious choice to act only after contemplating all aspects of matters as widely as possible. Be responsible, think and then act.

Only then we can make sure that we did our best to provide a healthy, humane and accepting society to our children - to the humans of the future.

In fact, you can only call yourself human, if you are responsible - if you are not responsible, then there is no difference between you and the rest of the animal kingdom, which inadvertently implies that you are not worthy of the honorable title of human.

Humanity is the highest of all forces. No technology - no science - no religion - is higher than humanity. All these forces can be tools in the hands of humanity, but they must never be taken to be the primary focus of humanity. The primary focus of humanity must always be placed on human life. Humanity first, nationality later - compassion first, religion later - acceptance first, formalities later.

And codes or algorithms or programs, no matter what you call it - the fact of the matter is, it is one of the most powerful tool that humankind has ever created with its own two hands. It is a potential - a force - a force without conscience, without character, without consciousness - so, it becomes our existential responsibility of gigantean proportions to make sure that we do not go mad over the possession of this power and keep using it willy-nilly as if it's a child's toy. It is our existential responsibility that, we sharpen our conscience to make sure that we are capable enough to use such a great power that we invented ourselves, quite accidentally if I might add, and pass on that responsibility to the young humans of tomorrow.

Codes are a force without character - so our character becomes their character. Technology is a force without character - so our character becomes its character. So, recklessness has no place in the use of technology, for such recklessness will only cause individual and collective degradation of an entire species.

Humans are lamentably insecure creatures, and often they pick up their modern devices to alleviate that insecurity, in a subconscious attempt to receive some thrill and reward. And the longer we keep on practicing such habit, the more hooked we get to our devices, often to the point of losing our mental stability. So, devices that were mainly invented as means of communication have become weapons of mental devastation.

Take the cameras on smartphones for example. The purpose of a camera is to capture memories, not replace them. Yet the unfortunate and rather ridiculous reality of today's so-called smart society is that, people have begun to place their focus on pictures instead of memories - they have already started to replace memories with pics - pics which in most cases have no emotional significance whatsoever. When they visit a new place, instead of embracing all the sweetness of that place with all their organic senses, they get busy taking selfies, so that they have tons of synthetic representations of their travel in their digital possession, even though those representations have very little memories in them.

I am pain-stricken to say, in an overwhelming attempt to capture memories, people have forgotten to make memories. The point is, your phone cannot tell you that taking tons of selfies are injurious to your health. You have to realize that yourself. Your phone won't remind you to actually keep it in your pocket as much as possible while visiting new places or meeting new people. You have to decide that yourself. Phones are neither good nor bad, they are just lifeless machines that were invented to serve humankind, yet humankind, with their ever-lasting stupidity have turned this communication marvel into psychological suicide.

Let me put it this way, today's humans do not need terrorists to disrupt peace in the world – they are doing it themselves quite well. Adorned with the unimaginable power of technology, regular people are disrupting peace in the society way more than terrorists do – they are disrupting peace both in their own lives as well the lives of others. And such acts are the product of reckless irresponsibility and incomprehensibility of the real impact of technological devices that are owned today by most of the human population.

If we put aside the mental health aspect, the devices that we own have turned almost every human on earth into a potential source of information, i.e. news, without the liability that goes with the term "news" in its traditional sense. Let me point out the gravitas of the matter, with an excerpt from one of my previous works "The Constitution of The United Peoples of Earth".

"Newspapers (and to a lesser extent magazines) have always been the primary medium of journalism since the 18th century, radio and television in the 20th century, and the Internet in the 21st century. However, more and more people are consuming news and other content from the internet than any other medium. And that's where the problem begins. The production and circulation of physical newspaper is highly expensive and so is maintaining a TV channel or a radio station, hence, transmission of news through these platforms are accessible mostly to traditional news media sources, and the public only acts as the consumer. But the same is not true when it comes to the transmission of news or any other content via the Internet. Anybody can transmit a news via the internet quite instantly as well as consume it. And since there is no active fact-checking algorithm involved in this transmission, there is no way of telling whether the news you are receiving is real or fake, if you are not receiving it from a trusted traditional source.

> However, since most of the traditional news publishing industry is hugely dependent on corporate sponsorship (except for a few publishers funded by people), even their news can be manipulated for the benefit of the sponsors or political lobbies. So, in the end, it all comes down to journalistic integrity - it comes down to the ethical grounds of the real conscientious journalists."

Therefore, it comes down to the matter of social trust upon the individual journalist, whose life purpose is to provide as much uninfluenced and unbiased information to the society as possible. The whole civilized world runs on trust - people trust journalists to provide accurate information, doctors to provide accurate treatment, scientists to provide accurate answers and solutions to unanswered questions and unsolved problems, pilots to provide safe and fast air transportation, and so on.

So, the integrity of the civilized world is predicated on the integrity of the individual in their chosen field of work. Upon their sense of responsibility depends the healthy functioning of an entire species. The integrity of the society is predicated on the integrity of each one of us. If you are responsible, if I am responsible, if we are responsible, then no matter how potent forces we hold in our hands, they can never be the weapons of destruction. We must stay awake at all times, because callousness would mean annihilation, first mental then physical.

Everyday Reality is Under Threat

Fake reality is not really something new. The reality we perceive is not the actual reality, it is subconsciously manufactured by the human brain based on our predominant biases, opinions, beliefs and instinctual drives. Likewise, deepfake is not the actual reality either - the only difference is that, deepfake is a reality which is consciously manufactured by humans to serve their conscious needs and interest.

Reality has really no direct relation to truth, unless we are primarily focused on the understanding of truth, like we do specifically in the world of science. And the most interesting part is, this construction of reality in the individual brain, based on its individual survival needs, takes place rather without the awareness of the individual. That's why often it's rather hard, if not impossible, for the individual to break free from their illusion of reality. The human population makes decisions, feels emotions and thinks thoughts, often rather subconsciously, without being aware of why they are doing so.

For example, in a study, a group of men were shown pictures of faces of different women. In half the photos the eyes of the women were dilated, and in the other half they were not. And when the men were asked to mention which faces looked more attractive to them, they consistently found the faces with dilated pupils more attractive, but they didn't have any clue as to the reason behind their decision. They simply felt more drawn to the faces with dilated pupils than others.

So, what's really happening here! Here, their brain gathered the data from the faces, including the tiny detail of dilated pupil and constructed the reality that the faces with dilated pupils were more attractive without the viewer even being aware of it. That's because to the brain, dilated pupils is a sign of sexual excitement and readiness. So, though the brain knows that there is a high probability that choosing women with dilated pupils over others would lead to reproductive success, it may not actually make that reason clear to the conscious mind of the individual. The conscious mind is only aware of the conclusion, not the data based on which the brain cooks up the conclusion.

The very notions of beauty and attractiveness are deeply hardwired within our neural circuits and they are meant to steer us in the right direction of survival. So most of our decisions are driven by subconscious programs carved by millions of years of natural selection. And the same goes for our very perception of reality.

Reality is constructed based on our own needs and knacks, especially those that our ancestors faced in their millions of years of existence in the jungle. This means that, we can go so far as to say that, reality and bias can often be seen as synonymous, because our biases create our reality in the pursuit of self-preservation, unless we make conscious and conscientious efforts to actually step beyond the biases as much as possible.

Now, that's the everyday kind of reality that we have been looking at. Now imagine the arrival of another kind of reality into the picture, where even the identity of people is no longer their exclusive possession. For example, if you see a public figure saying something obnoxious on television or on the internet, you automatically begin to make opinions on that public figure.

Now here is the interesting part. Till now, we didn't have the technology to doctor videos or audios flawlessly, but now with deepfake technology we do. Which means, the very line between real and unreal as we have known for so far, no longer holds any value. To put it simply, if you watch a video or listen to an audio of someone saying or doing something, you have no way of telling whether that act or that comment has really been made by that person.

For example, in an attempt to ruin my reputation in the society, if some extremist group makes a video of me forcefully trying to have sex with a woman and puts it up on the internet, you literally have no way of not believing that it's me. And while there is nothing wrong with having sex (pedophilia, infidelity, promiscuity excluded), consent is the line between human behavior and bestiality. Suddenly all my words and ideas would turn meaningless in your eyes. The only thing that may - just may - keep you from not believing your eyes, is your understanding of my work. However, that's exactly the kind of world we are heading towards, where anyone can cook up any kind of video of someone to ruin their reputation. And I mean this literally.

Think about when you try to photoshop your picture to add a new background. Now, you can only create a flawless image of you on top of the Everest, if you are a photoshop expert, otherwise, you will end up with a picture of the Everest with your cropped figure placed on top it. If you are a photoshop expert, people would have no reason not to believe that you've climbed the Mount Everest. But if you are not an expert, then everybody would simply know that you tried your hands on photoshop.

This photoshopping phenomenon on pictures has been going on for some time now. But it's only recently that we have developed the technology to do the same with video and audio with exceptionally realistic details. This is not just computer graphics - it's much more than that. In fact, over time deepfakes will only make computer graphics generation more realistic and affordable, as artificial intelligence begins to do most of the editing.

But this also means that the porn industry is about to witness a booming of deepfake generated videos, which will directly affect not only public figures, but regular people, especially teenagers. So far there is no way of stopping deepfake from being used in the generation of so-called revenge porn.

The point is, there are many people including some of my close friends and colleagues who are making all the efforts possible to hold the creators of artificial intelligence algorithms legally accountable for their impact on the society with policies and regulations, but the fact of the matter is, once the source code of a program is made public, which is called open-source, there is no way of keeping people from using it to serve their own purpose - in fact, even if the source code of a program is not made public, if it holds potential, sooner or later someone always replicates it.

Therefore, alongside making everything possible to hold the creators of the artificial intelligence algorithms liable, we must also keep in mind that we will not succeed in stopping AI programs, like deepfakes from being used for destructive purposes. It's a genie that we have let loose in the world, now no matter how much we try to put it back in the bottle, we can't. Keeping this in mind, we must proceed. We must raise our children with all the courage we can muster so that they can tackle the dark side of technology without committing suicide. And I mean this literally.

Modern humans are taught from the childhood that they are weak and sinners. But we don't have the primitive luxury to do that anymore, because the whole societal structure is about to get more messed up than it ever was in the 3.5 billion years long history of life on this planet. In such a society, where the very concept of reality is fragile and unstable, the humans would need all the courage and character they can muster.

Once a baby is born, the parents have around one and a half decades to build his or her character and fill the mind with vigour and virtues. So, teach them that they are embodiment of glory and children of immortal strength. Eventually a society full of bravehearts will rise. Never put a single thought of weakness in the flourishing minds of the children. Fill them up with vigour and compassion, for their character will define the future of the entire human species. Feed your child ideas of peace, harmony and compassion but at the same time give them courage to defend their identity and dignity.

We no longer have the naïve luxury to raise chickens seeking security all through their life, because we have with our own recklessness created a world where the very idea of security is going to be challenged every step of the way. So, muster all the courage and conscience and raise bravehearts of character. Remember, the only qualities that will enable the humans to pass through the forthcoming turbulence and instability are courage and character.

Progress without Health
is Abuse of Potential

What happens to our world is personal to all of us - and it must be taken as such, for if you think that the problems of this world are none of your business or that they don't affect you directly, then you couldn't be more foolishly deluded. While it is true that many of the problems of our world may not affect us directly and instantly, but they unavoidably will have direct implications in the life our children and grandchildren.

Now, you may shut your eyes with the veil of indifference and reckless callousness, but that won't stop the coming generations to be disgusted at your stupidity. You have two choices - either do nothing and be the object of shame and disgust for your children or stand up and act, so that the coming humans take pride in you and above all, learn the greatest lesson of life from you - the lesson of responsibility.

Remember, if our children grow up to be irresponsible, reckless, self-obsessed, materialist, shallow snobs with no content of character, it'll not be their fault, but ours. So, though every generation must chisel their own destiny, it is our responsibility, as not just civilized adults, but as conscientious humans of the global society, that we sow the seeds of humility, amity and humanity in the soil of their flourishing psyche.

We need more country than concrete, we need more mind than material, we need more savannah than sky-scrapers, we need more melody than malady. And this can only happen if we make simplicity and responsibility the way of life. Solace is in simplicity. Over-abundance of technology won't ensure the health and prosperity of our species, what will is our responsible use of that technology.

In fact, technology will destroy this planet mentally, if responsible individuals do not come forward to advocate for responsible use of technology. Be responsible, because irresponsibility means annihilation - annihilation of the two fundamental elements of human existence, without which all external progress turns worthless - serenity and sanity.

Serenity and sanity have already become scarce in our so-called advanced human society. Our pursuit of instant gratifications and instant progress has been leading us down the path of mental deterioration and we seem to be completely unaware of it. And if this continues, then soon serenity will become the most expensive commodity in the market - which will be sold to everyone by the pharmaceutical industry in the form of pills and treatments.

Now here, please do not consider me as some anti-medicine advocate, because I am not. I am a scientist and my work is to point to you the direction in which we are going. Medicine has its place in treating illnesses, but when the mind becomes completely incapable to sustaining peace and sanity within itself without the aid of pills, then it is a matter of great concern - in fact, the very possibility is horrifying. Is that the future you have in mind for your children, where their diet will contain more pills than food? To them mental health, or simply "peace of mind" will be an alien concept, which they would have classes and debates about, but without any practical realization or understanding of the matter.

To understand mental health, we must first understand what is mind? And by understand, I mean realize, in our bones, what this mind thing is. So, let's try to figure out. I assume you know what water is – what it is made of. It's made of hydrogen and oxygen. That's why, water is H2O. Likewise, mind is made of neurons – most of which are inside our brain and the rest are spread across our body like a network, not just to drive our body, but also to receive information from the environment. And what we call consciousness is only the surface of the mind.

Like the rest of the mind, consciousness is the product of electrochemical signalling in the neurons of your brain. So when the brain stops functioning fully, your consciousness, or to a broader aspect your mind ceases to exist with its unique individualistic qualities. It's like the soothing flow of water. It is only water as long as its internal realm of two atoms of hydrogen and one atom of oxygen, remains intact. If you break that structure which we call H20, it ceases to be water. Likewise, a mind remains a mind, as long as its neural structure remains intact. If you mess with this structure, then the entire personality of the mind may get radically altered. And if the neural structure inside your head stops working, then your mind ceases to exist forever. So, as long as you have a functional brain, you exist, and the moment that brain dies you die.

We have about a hundred billion neurons in our brain. And just so you know, the number of neurons remains almost the same since the time of our birth, what changes as we grow up and live through time, is their interconnections. For example, when you practice a certain task over a long period of time, the neurons responsible for that task, get substantially interconnected, and as they get more interconnected, you become better at that task.

Now, where does mental health come in all this? Well you see, we are all animals. Yes we are, technically speaking. But since we severed our dependency on Mother Nature, by building civilizations - modern civilizations, we became somewhat non-animal. Which means, we no longer rely on the internal mechanisms that helped up animals to survive in the jungle alongside other animals. And these mechanisms are what we call instincts. But by instincts, I am not talking about the way you use the term in everyday life. I am not talking about just gut feeling. Instinctual drives helped us survive in the merciless kingdom of the wild – the drive for reproduction, the drive for staying alert and so on.

Now, the drive for staying alert is the instinct that's responsible for most of our modern everyday mental health issues – anxieties, stress and so on. Why, because we are not wired in our brain to stay calm – we are not wired to remain peaceful – we come from a long line of ancestors, who had to remain alert all the time, in order to be able to fight any possible predatory attack. And this evolutionary instinct of alertness still remains quite strong in the human psyche, except now, we have labeled it with problematic terms like anxiety, stress and so on.

We have started to delude ourselves with the belief that these everyday mental health issues are our enemies that have risen recently, but the truth is quite the opposite. As I have said in one of my previous works - fear, anxiety, stress, these are not our enemies. You cannot get rid of them, by thinking of them as enemies. They are a form of evolutionary wisdom in the face of danger. So, you should not try to get rid of them, rather you should try to befriend them.

Accept them as part of your life – accept them as part of your being – rid yourself of the fairytale notion, that you ought to be full of happiness all the time – rid yourself of the false belief that being sad is bad, that being upset or disappointed is bad – these are all human conditions – one can't erase them, just because one doesn't like them or one's society presents them as evil. Only when you accept yourself, the way you are, with all your joys, sorrows, miseries, disappointments, failures, achievements and ecstasies, can you truly step beyond the dualities of existence – only then can you become truly alive to life itself.

Mental health awareness doesn't mean fighting stress, anxiety, depression and other everyday mental health issues, rather it means consciously modulating the habits that intensify those issues. Once you are in control of your habits, instead of letting your habits control you, you would automatically be in a much better shape, both mentally and physically.

In fact, if we put aside the severe neuropsychological conditions, there is no such thing as mental health awareness, there is only awareness. Awareness breeds health, whereas callousness breeds more suffering. Awareness also breeds insight into the right place of progress in the human society.

In a truly civilized and sapient society, health and progress go hand in hand. Malfunction of either one would mean an absolute collapse of the sweet everyday ordinary societal fabric. Health without progress is potential unused, whereas, progress without health is potential abused.

Progress doesn't mean building skyscraper after skyscraper – progress doesn't mean innovating machine after machine – these can indeed be the tell-tale signs of a progressive society, but if the people living in those skyscrapers and using those machines do not have the plain ordinary everyday sweetness in their life, then such a progress is of consequence. The measure of progress is not in how many smart cities we've built, or how many revolutionary technologies we've invented – the measure of progress is in how many lives we've improved.

BIBLIOGRAPHY

Archer M., (2000), Being Human: The Problem of Agency. Cambridge University Press.

Archer M., (2003), Structure, Agency and the Internal Conversation. Cambridge University Press.

Adolphs R (2003) Cognitive neuroscience of human social behaviour. Nature Rev Neurosci 4: 165–178.

Adolphs R, Tranel D, Damasio AR (2003) Dissociable neural systems for recognizing emotions. Brain Cogn 52: 61–69.

Afton, A. D. (1985). Forced copulation as a reproductive strategy of male lesser scaup: A field test of some predictions. - Behaviour 92, p. 146-167.

Allison T, Puce A, McCarthy G. (2000) Social perception from visual cues: role of the STS region. Trends Cogn Sci 4: 267–278.

Andresen, Jensine, and Robert Forman, eds. Cognitive Models and Spiritual Maps. Bowling Green, Ohio: Imprint Academic, 2000.

Ashbrook, James, and Carol Albright. The Humanizing Brain: Where Religion and Neuroscience Meet. Cleveland, OH: Pilgrim Press, 1997.

Azari, Nina, Janpeter Nickel, Gilbert Wunderlich, Michael Niedeggen, Harald Hefter, Lutz Tellmann, Hans Herzog, Petra Stoerig, Dieter Birnbacher, and Rudiger Seitz. "Neural Correlates of Religious Experience." European Journal of Neuroscience 13, no. 8 (2001)

Agar, N. (2004). Liberal eugenics: In defence of human enhancement. London: Blackwell Publishing.

Alteheld, N., Roessler, G., Vobig, M., & Walter, R. (2004). The retina implant new approach to a visual prosthesis. Biomedizinische Technik, 49(4), 99–103.

Antal, A., Nitsche, M. A., Kincses, T. Z., Kruse, W., Hoffmann, K. P., & Paulus, W. (2004a). Facilitation of visuo-motor learning by transcranial direct current stimulation of the motor and extrastriate visual areas in humans. European Journal of Neuroscience, 19(10), 2888–2892.

Bhat Z, Kumar, S, Bhat H (2015) In vitro meat production. Challenges and benefits over conventional meat production. J Sci Food Agric 14: 241–248

Bernstein R. J., (1967), John Dewey. New York: Washington Square Press.

Bernstein R.J., (1971), Praxis and Action: Contemporary Philosophies of Human Activity. Philadelphia: University of Pennsylvania Press.

Bernstein R.J., (1976), The Restructuring Social and Political Thought.

Bernstein R.J., (1983), Beyond Relativism and Objectivism: Science, Hermeneutics, and Praxis. Philadelphia: University of Pennsylvania Press.

Bernstein R.J., (1986), Philosophical Profiles. Philadelphia: University of Pennsylvania Press.

Bernstein R.J., (1991), New Constellation. Cambridge: MIT Press.

Barash, D. P. (1977). Sociobiology of rape in mallards (Anas platyrhynchos): Responses of the mated male. - Science 197, p. 788-789.

Berger, J. (1986). Wild horses of the great basin: Social competition and population size. - The University of Chicago Press, Chicago.

Birkhead, T. R., Johnson, S. D. & Nettleship, D. N. (1985). Extra-pair matings and mate guarding in the common murre Uria aalge. - Anim. Behav. 33, p. 608-619.

Beauregard, Mario, and Vincent Paquette. "Neural Correlates of a Mystical Experience in Carmelite Nuns." Neuroscience Letters 405, no. 3 (2006)

Benson, Herbert. Timeless Healing: The Power and Biology of Belief. New York: Scribner, 1996

Bogen, J.E.(1995a), 'On the neurophysiology of consciousness: Part I. An overview', Consciousness and Cognition, 4.

Bogen, J.E. (1995b), 'On the neurophysiology of consciousness: Part II. Constraining the semantic problem', Consciousness and Cognition, 4.

Bremner, J. D., R. Soufer, et al. (2001). "Gender differences in cognitive and neural correlates of remembrance of emotional words." Psychopharmacol Bull 35 (3).

Brothers, L. (2002). The social brain: A project for integrating primate behavior and neurophysiology in a new domain. In J. T. Cacioppo et al. (Eds.), Foundations in neuroscience. Cambridge, MA: MIT Press.

Buss, D. D. (2003). Evolutionary Psychology: The New Science of Mind, 2nd ed. New York: Allyn & Bacon.

Buss, D. M. (1989). "Conflict between the sexes: Strategic interference and the evocation of anger and upset." J Pers Soc Psychol 56 (5).

Buss, D. M. (1995). "Psychological sex differences. Origins through sexual selection." Am Psychol 50 (3).

Buss, D. M. (2002). "Review: Human Mate Guarding." Neuro Endocrinol Lett 23 (Suppl 4).

Buss, D. M., and D. P. Schmitt (1993). "Sexual strategies theory: An evolutionary perspective on human mating." Psychol Rev 100 (2).

Blakemore SJ, Decety J (2001) From the perception of action to the understanding of intention. Nature Rev Neurosci 2: 561.

Bruce C, Desimone R, Gross CG (1981) Visual properties of neurons in a polysensory area in superior temporal sulcus of the macaque. J Neurophysiol 46: 369–384.

Buccino G, Vogt S, Ritzl A, Fink GR, Zilles K, Freund HJ, Rizzolatti G (2004) Neural circuits underlying imitation of hand actions: an event related fMRI study. Neuron 42: 323–34.

Colapietro V., (1988), "Human Agency: The Habits of Our Being."

Southern Journal of Philosophy, XXVI, 2, pp. 153-68.

Colapietro V., (1992), "Purpose, Power, and Agency." The Monist, 75, 4 (October) pp. 423-44.

Colapietro V., (2003), "Signs and their vicissitudes: Meanings in excess of consciousness and functionality." Logica, Dialogica, Ideologica, a cure di Susan Petrilli e Patrizia Calefato (Milano: Mimesis), pp. 221-36.

Colapietro V., (2004a), "C. S. Peirce's Reclamation of Teleology." Nature in American Philosophy, ed. Jean De Groot (Washington, D.C.: Catholic University Press of America), pp. 88-108.

Colapietro V., (2004b), "Portrait of a Historicist: An Alternative Reading of Peircean Semiotic." Semiotiche, 2/04 [maggio 2004], pp. 49-68.

Colapietro V., (2006), "Engaged Pluralism: Between Alterity and

Sociality." The Pragmatic Century: Conversations with Richard J. Bernstein (Albany, NY: SUNY Press), pp. 39-68.

Colapietro V., (2009), "Habit, Competence, and Purpose." Forthcoming in The Transactions of the Charles S. Peirce Society. Calder AJ, Keane J, Manes F, Antoun N, Young AW (2000) Impaired recognition and experience of disgust following brain injury. Nature Neurosci 3: 1077–1078.

Carey DP, Perrett DI, Oram MW (1997) Recognizing, understanding and reproducing actions. In: Jeannerod M, Grafman J (eds) Handbook of neuropsychology. Vol. 11: Action and cognition. Elsevier, Amsterdam.

Carr L, Iacoboni M, Dubeau MC, Mazziotta JC, Lenzi GL (2003) Neural mechanisms of empathy in humans: a relay from neural systems for imitation to limbic areas. Proc Natl Acad Sci USA 100: 5497–5502.

Changeux JP, Ricoeur P (1998) La nature et la règle. Odile Jacob, Paris.

Cochin S, Barthelemy C, Roux S, Martineau J (1999) Observation and execution of movement: similarities demonstrated by quantified electroencephalograpy. Eur J Neurosci 11: 1839– 1842.

Chomsky Noam, (2017) Requiem for the American Dream

Chomsky Noam, (2016) Who Rules the World?

Chomsky Noam, (2010) How the World Works

Churchland, P.S. (1986), Neurophilosophy (Cambridge, MA: The MIT Press).

Churchland, P.S. & Ramachandran, V.S. (1993), 'Filling in: Why Dennett is wrong', in Dennett and His Critics:

Demystifying Mind, ed. B. Dahlbom (Oxford: Blackwell Scientific Press).

Churchland, P.S., Ramachandran, V.S. & Sejnowski, T.J. (1994), 'A critique of pure vision', in Large- scale Neuronal Theories of the Brain, ed. C. Koch & J.L. Davis (Cambridge, MA: The MIT Press).

Crick, F. (1994), The Astonishing Hypothesis: The Scientific Search for the Soul (New York: Simon and Schuster).

Crick, F. (1996), 'Visual perception: rivalry and consciousness', Nature, 379.

Crick, F. & Koch, C. (1992), 'The problem of consciousness', Scientific American, 267.

Craig AD (2002) How do you feel? Interoception: the sense of the physiological condition of the body. Nature Rev Neurosci 3: 655–666.

Damasio, A (2003a) Looking for Spinoza. Harcourt Inc. Damasio A (2003b) Feeling of emotion and the self. Ann NY Acad Sci 1001: 253–261.

d'Aquili, Eugene. "Senses of Reality in Science and Religion." Zygon 17, no 4 (1982)

d'Aquili, Eugene. "The Biopsychological Determinants of Religious Ritual Behavior." Zygon 10, no. 1 (1975)

d'Aquili, Eugene. "The Myth-Ritual Complex: A Biogenetic Structural Analysis." Zygon 18, no. 3 (1983)

d'Aquili, Eugene, and Andrew Newberg. The Mystical Mind: Probing the Biology of Religious Experience. Minneapolis: Fortress Press, 1999.

Daly DD. 1958. Ictal affect. Am J Psychiatry.

Damasio, A. (1994) Descartes' Error: Emotion, Reason and the Human Brain. New York, Putnams.

Damasio, A. (1999) The Feeling of What Happens: Body, Emotion and the Making of Consciousness. London, Heinemann.

Darwin, C. (1859) On the Origin of Species by Means of Natural Selection. London, Murray.

Darwin, C. (1871) The Descent of Man and Selection in Relation to Sex. London, John Murray.

Darwin, C. (1872) The Expression of the Emotions in Man and Animals. London, John Murray; also published 1965, Chicago, University of Chicago Press.

Dawkins, M.S. (1987) Minding and mattering. In C. Blakemore and S. Greenfield (eds) Mindwaves. Oxford, Blackwell, 151-60.

Dawkins, R. (1976) The Selfish Gene. Oxford, Oxford University Press; a new edition, with additional material, was published in 1989.

Dawkins, R. (1986) The Blind Watchmaker. London, Longman.

Di Pellegrino G, Fadiga L, Fogassi L, Gallese V, Rizzolatti G (1992) Understanding motor events: A neurophysiological study. Exp Brain Res 91: 176–80.

Deikman, A.J. (2000) A functional approach to mysticism. Journal of Consciousness Studies 7(11-12), 75-91.

Delmonte, M.M. (1987) Personality and meditation. In M. West (ed.) The Psychology of Meditation. Oxford, Clarendon Press, 118-32.

Dennett, D.C. (1987) The Intentional Stance. Cambridge, MA, MIT Press.

Dennett, D.C. (1988) Quining qualia. In A.J. Marcel and E. Bisiach (eds)

Consciousness in Contemporary Science. Oxford, Oxford University Press, 42-77.

Dennett, D.C. (1991) Consciousness Explained. Boston, MA, and London, Little, Brown and Co.

Dennett, D.C. (1995a) Darwin's Dangerous Idea. London, Penguin.

Dennett, D.C. (1995b) The unimagined preposterousness of zombies. Journal of Consciousness Studies 2(4), 322-6.

Dennett, D.C. (1995c) Cog: steps towards consciousness in robots. In T. Metzinger (ed.) Conscious Experience. Thorverton, Devon, Imprint Academic, 471-87.

Dennett, D.C. (1995d) The path not taken. Behavioral and Brain Sciences 18, 252-3; commentary on N. Block, On a confusion about a function of consciousness. Behavioral and Brain Sciences 18, 227.

Dennett, D.C. (1996a) Facing backwards on the problem of consciousness. Journal of Consciousness Studies 3(1), 4-6.

Dennett, D.C. (1996b) Kinds of Minds: Towards an Understanding of Consciousness. London, Weidenfeld & Nicolson.

Dennett, D.C. (1997) An exchange with Daniel Dennett. In J. Searle (ed.) The Mystery of Consciousness. New York, New York Review of Books, 115-19.

Dennett, D.C. (1998) The myth of double transduction. In S.R. Hameroff, A.W. Kaszniak and A. C. Scott (eds) Toward a Science of Consciousness: The Second Tucson Discussions and Debates. Cambridge, MA, MIT Press, 97-107.

Dennett, D.C. (1998b) Brainchildren: Essays on Designing Minds. Cambridge, MA, MIT Press.

Dennett, D.C. (2001) The fantasy of first person science. Debate with D. Chalmers, Northwestern University, Evanston, IL, February 2001.

Dennett, D.C. (2003) Freedom Evolves. New York, Penguin.

Dennett, D.C. and Kinsbourne, M. (1992) Time and the observer: the where and when of consciousness in the brain. Behavioral and Brain Sciences 15, 183-247, including commentaries and authors' responses.

Dewey J., (1911 [1977]), "Epistemological Realism: The Alleged Ubiquity of the Knowledge Relation." Journal of Philosophy, VIII, 20 (September 28, 1911).

Dewhurst, Kenneth, and A. W. Beard. "Sudden Religious Conversions in Temporal Lobe Epilepsy." British Journal of Psychiatry 117 (1970)

Dewhurst K, Beard AW. Sudden religious conversions in temporal lobe epilepsy. 1970 Epilepsy Behav 2003

Devinsky O, Lai G. Spirituality and religion in epilepsy. Epilepsy Behav 2008.

Devinsky, O., Morrell, MJ, Vogt, BA. (1995) 'Contribution of anterior cingulate cortex to behavior', Brain, 118.

Douglas Stone A., Chapter 24, The Indian Comet, in the book Einstein and the Quantum, Princeton University Press, Princeton, New Jersey, 2013.

E. Horvitz, "One Hundred Year Study on Artificial Intelligence: Reflections and Framing," ed: Stanford University, 2014.

Einstein A. (1925). "Quantentheorie des einatomigen idealen Gases". Sitzungsberichte der Preussischen Akademie der Wissenschaften.

Eckhart Meister, Selected Writings

Egidi R., ed. (1999), "Von Wright and 'Dante's Dream': Stages in a Philosophical Pilgrim's Progress", in In Search of a New Humanism: the Philosophy of G.H. von Wright, ed. by R. Egidi, Kluwer, Dordrecht.

Fadiga L, Fogassi L, Pavesi G, Rizzolatti G (1995) Motor facilitation during action observation: a magnetic stimulation study. J Neurophysiol 73: 2608–2611.

Fogassi L, Gallese V, Fadiga L, Rizzolatti G (1998) Neurons responding to the sight of goal directed hand/arm actions in the parietal area PF (7b) of the macaque monkey. Soc Neurosci Abs 24:257.5.

Frith U, Frith CD (2003) Development and neurophysiology of mentalizing. Philos Trans R Soc Lond B Biol Sci 358: 459.

Farah, M.J. (1989), 'The neural basis of mental imagery', Trends in Neurosciences, 10.

Finlay BL, Darlington RB (1995) Linked regularities in the development and evolution of mammalian brains. Science 268.

Freud, S. "The Interpretation of Dreams", 1900

Freud, S. "Selected papers on hysteria and other psychoneuroses" Journal of Nervous and Mental Disease 1909.

Freud, S. "The Origin and Development of Psychoanalysis", 1910

Freud, S. "Psychopathology of everyday life", 1914

Freud, S. "Beyond the Pleasure Principle", 1920

Frith, C.D. & Dolan, R.J. (1997), 'Abnormal beliefs: Delusions and memory', Paper presented at the May,

1997, Harvard Conference on Memory and Belief.

Gay, Volney, ed. Neuroscience and Religion. Plymouth, UK: Lexington Books, 2009.

Gazzaniga, M. S. (1985). The social brain. New York: Basic Books.

Gazzaniga, M.S. (1993), 'Brain mechanisms and conscious experience', Ciba Foundation Symposium, 174.

Geschwind N. "Behavioural changes in temporal lobe epilepsy". Psychol Med. 1979.

Gellhorn, E., Kiely, W.F. "Mystical states of consciousness: neurophysiological and clinical aspects." J Nerv Ment Dis. 1972;154:399-405.

Gilbert SL, Dobyns WB, Lahn BT (2005) Genetic links between brain development and brain evolution. Nat Rev Genet 6.

Gray JA. The Psychology of Fear and Stress. 2nd ed. New York, NY: Cambridge University Press; 1988.

Gloor, P. (1992), 'Amygdala and temporal lobe epilepsy', in The Amygdala: Neurobiological Aspects of Emotion, Memory and Mental Dysfunction, ed J.P. Aggleton (New York: Wiley-Liss).

Greenspan, S. I. and S. G. Shanker (2004). The first idea: How symbols, language, and intelligence evolved from our early primate ancestors to modern humans. Cambridge, MA: Da Capo Press.

Grady, D. (1993), 'The vision thing: Mainly in the brain', Discover, June.

Gallagher HL, Frith CD (2003) Functional imaging of 'theory of mind'. Trends Cogn Sci 7: 77.

Gallese V, Fogassi L, Fadiga L, Rizzolatti G (2002) Action representation and the inferior parietal lobule. In: Prinz W, Hommel B (eds) Attention & Performance XIX. Common mechanisms in perception and action. Oxford University Press, Oxford.

Gallese V, Keysers C, Rizzolatti G (2004) A unifying view of the basis of social cognition. Trends Cogn Sci 8: 396–403.

Gangitano M, Mottaghy FM, Pascual-Leone A (2001) Phase specific modulation of cortical motor output during movement observation. NeuroReport 12: 1489–1492.

Gangitano M, Mottaghy FM, Pascual-Leone A (2004) Modulation of premotor mirror neuron activity during observation of unpredictable grasping movements. Eur J Neurosci 20: 2193– 2202.

Goldman AI, Sripada CS (2004) Simulationist models of face-based emotion recognition. Cognition 94: 193–213.

Grèzes J, Costes N, Decety J (1998) Top-down effect of strategy on the perception of human biological motion: a PET investigation. Cogn Neuropsychol 15: 553–582.

Grèzes J, Armony JL, Rowe J, Passingham RE (2003) Activations related to "mirror" and "canonical" neurones in the human brain: an fMRI study. Neuroimage 18: 928–937.

Gross CG, Rocha-Miranda CE, Bender DB (1972) Visual properties of neurons in the inferotemporal cortex of the macaque. J Neurophysiol 35: 96–111.

Hari R, Forss N, Avikainen S, Kirveskari S, Salenius S, Rizzolatti G (1998) Activation of human primary motor cortex during action observation: a neuromagnetic study.

Proc. Natl Acad Sci USA 95: 15061–15065.

Hardy, G. H. (1940). Ramanujan. Cambridge: Cambridge University Press.

Hall, Daniel, Keith Meador, and Harold Koenig. "Measuring Religiousness in Health Research: Review and Critique." Journal of Religion and Health 47, no. 2 (2008)

Harris, Sam, Jonas Kaplan, Ashley Curiel, Susan Bookheimer, Marco Iacoboni, and Mark Cohen. "The Neural Correlates of Religious and Nonreligious Belief." PLoS One 4, no. 10 (October 1, 2009)

Halgren, E. (1992), 'Emotional neurophysiology of the amygdala within the context of human cognition', in The Amygdala: Neurobiological Aspects of Emotion, Memory and Mental Dysfunction, ed J.P. Aggleton (New York: Wiley-Liss).

Halligan PW, Fink GR, Marshal JC, Vallar G. 2003. Spatial cognition: evidence from visual neglect. Trends Cogn Sci.

Handbook of Emotions, Edited by Michael Lewis, Jeannette M. Haviland-Jones, and Lisa Feldman Barrett, The Guilford Press; 3rd edition (2010).

Haggard, P., Clark, S. and Kalogeras,]. (2002) Voluntary action and conscious awareness, Nature Neuroscience 5, 382-5. Haggard, P., Newman, C. and Magno, E. (1999) On the perceived time of voluntary actions. British Journal of Psychology 90, 291-303.

Hameroff, S.R. and Penrose, R. (1996) Conscious events as orchestrated space-time selections. Journal of Consciousness Studies 3(1), 36-53; also reprinted in J. Shear (ed.) (1997) Explaining Consciousness-The Hard Problem. Cambridge, MA, MIT Press, 177-95.

Hardcastle, V.G. (2000) How to understand theN in NCC. InT. Metzinger (ed.) Neural Correlates of Consciousness. Cambridge, MA, MIT Press, 259-64.

Harding, D.E. (1961) On Having no Head: Zen and the Re-Discovery of the Obvious. London, Buddhist Society.

Hardy, A. (1979) The Spiritual Nature of Man: A Study of Contemporary Religious Experience. Oxford, Clarendon Press.

Hamad, S. (1990) The symbol grounding problem. Physica D 42, 335-46.

Hamad, S. (2001) No easy way out. The Sciences 41(2), 36-42.

Harre, R. and Gillett, G. (1994) The Discursive Mind. Thousand Oaks, CA, Sage.

Haugeland, J. (ed.) (1997) Mind Design II: Philosophy, Psychology, Artificial

Intelligence. Cambridge, MA, MIT Press.

Hauser, M.D. (2000) Wild Minds: What Animals Really Think. New York, Henry Holt and Co.; London, Penguin.

Hearne, K. (1990) The Dream Machine. Northants, Aquarian.

Hebb, D.O. (1949) The Organization of Behavior. New York, Wiley.

Helmholtz, H.L.F. von (1856-67) Treatise on Physiological Optics.

Hess, EH (1975) "The role of pupil size in communication," Scientific American, 233(5), 110–12.

Heyes, C.M. (1998) Theory of mind in nonhuman primates. Behavioral and Brain Sciences 21, 101-48; with commentaries.

Heyes, C.M. and Galef, B.G. (eds) (1996) Social Learning in Animals: The Roots of Culture. San Diego, CA, Academic Press.

Hilgard, E.R. (1986) Divided Consciousness: Multiple Controls in Human Thought and Action. New York, Wiley.

Hocquette JF (2016) Is in vitro meat the solution for the future? Meat Science 120:

167–176

Hodgson, R. (1891) A case of double consciousness. Proceedings of the Society for Psychical Research 7, 221-58.

Hofstadter, D.R. (1979) Code!, Escher, Bach: An Eternal Golden Braid. London, Penguin.

Hofstadter, D.R. and Dennett, D.C. (eds) (1981) The Mind's I: Fantasies and Reflections on Self and Soul. London, Penguin.

Holland, J. (ed.) (2001) Ecstasy: The Complete Guide: A Comprehensive Look at the Risks and Benefits of

MDMA. Rochester, VT, Park Street Press.

Holmes, D.S. (1987) The influence of meditation versus rest on physiological arousal. In M. West (ed.) The Psychology of Meditation. Oxford, Clarendon Press, 81-103.

Holt, J. (1999) Blindsight in debates about qualia. Journal of Consciousness Studies 6(5), 54-71.

Horgan, J. (1994), 'Can science explain consciousness?', Scientific American, 271.

Holloway RL (1996) Evolution of the human brain. In: Lock A, Peters CR (eds) Handbook of human symbolic evolution. Oxford University Press, Oxford

Iacoboni M, Woods RP, Brass M, Bekkering H, Mazziotta JC, Rizzolatti G (1999) Cortical mechanisms of human imitation. Science 286: 2526–2528.

Iacoboni M, Koski LM, Brass M, Bekkering H, Woods RP, Dubeau MC, Mazziotta JC, Rizzolatti G (2001) Reafferent copies of imitated actions in the right superior temporal cortex. Proc Natl Acad Sci USA 98: 13995–13999.

Jeannerod M (1988) The neural and behavioural organization of goal-directed movements. Clarendon Press, Oxford.

Johnson-Frey SH, Maloof FR, Newman-Norlund R, Farrer C, Inati S, Grafton ST (2003) Actions or hand-objects interactions? Human inferior frontal cortex and action observation. Neuron 39: 1053–1058.

Jackson, F. (1982) Epiphenomenal qualia. Philosophical Quarterly 32, 127-36.

James, W. (1890) The Principles of Psychology (2 volumes). London, Macmillan.

James, W. (1902) The Varieties of Religious Experience: A Study in Human Nature. New York and London, Longmans, Green and Co.

Jansen, K. (2001) Ketamine: Dreams and Realities. Sarasota, FL, Multidisciplinary Association for Psychedelic Studies.

Jay, M. (ed.) (1999) Artificial Paradises: A Drugs Reader. London, Penguin.

Jaynes, J. (1976) The Origin of Consciousness in the Breakdown of the Bicameral Mind. New York, Houghton Mifflin.

Johnson, M.K. and Raye, C.L. (1981) Reality monitoring. Psychological Review 88, 67-85.

Kadim I, Mahgoub O, Baqir S et al. (2015) Cultured meat from muscle stem cells: a review of challenges and prospects. J Integr Agr 14: 222–233

Koski L, Iacoboni M, Dubeau MC, Woods RP, Mazziotta JC (2003) Modulation of cortical activity during different imitative behaviors. J Neurophysiol 89: 460–471.

Krolak-Salmon P, Henaff MA, Isnard J, Tallon-Baudry C, Guenot M, Vighetto A, Bertrand O, Mauguiere F (2003) An attention modulated response to disgust in human ventral anterior insula. Ann Neurol 53: 446–453.

Kandel, E. R. In Search of Memory: The Emergence of a New Science of Mind, W. W. Norton & Company (2007).

Kandel E. R. Schwartz JH, Jessel TM. Principles of neural sciences. New York; McGraw Hill, 2000.

Kanizsa, G. (1979), Organization In Vision (New York: Praeger).

Kaloupek DG, Scott JR, Khatami V. Assessment of coping strategies associated with syncope in blood donors. J Psychosom Res. 1985;29:207-214.

Kanwisher, N. (2001) Neural events and perceptual awareness. Cognition 79, 89-113; also reprinted inS. Dehaene (ed.) The Cognitive Neuroscience of Consciousness. Cambridge, MA, MIT Press, 89-113.

Kapleau, Roshi P. (1980) The Three Pillars of Zen: Teaching, Practice, and Enlightenment (revised edn). New York, Doubleday.

Karn, K. and Hayhoe, M. (2000) Memory representations guide targeting eye movements in a natural task. Visual Cognition 7, 673-703.

Kasamatsu, A. and Hirai, T. (1966) An electroencephalographic study on the Zen meditation (zazen). Folia Psychiatrica et Neurologica Japonica 20, 315-36.

Kaiserman-Abramof, I. R., Graybiel, A. M., & Nauta, W. J. (1980). The thalamic projection to cortical area 17 in a congenitally anophthalmic mouse strain. Neuroscience, 5, 41–52.

Kanold, P. O., Kara, P., Reid, R. C., & Shatz, C. J. (2003). Role of subplate neurons in functional maturation of visual cortical columns. Science, 301, 521–525.

Kennedy, H., & Dehay, C. (1988). Functional implications of the anatomical organization of the callosal projections of visual areas V1 and V2 in the macaque monkey. Behav. Brain Res., 29, 225–236.

Kentridge, R.W. and Heywood, C.A. (1999) The status of blindsight. Journal of Consciousness Studies 6(5), 3-11.

Kihlstrom, J.F. (1996) Perception without awareness of what is perceived, learning without awareness of what is learned. In M. Velmans (ed.) The Science of Consciousness. London, Routledge, 23-46.

Kollerstrom, N. (1999) The path of Halley's comet, and Newton's late apprehension of the law of gravity. Annals of Science 56, 331-56.

Kosslyn, S.M. (1980) Image and Mind. Cambridge, MA, Harvard University Press.

Kosslyn, S.M. (1988) Aspects of a cognitive neuroscience of mental imagery. Science 240, 1621-6.

Kinsbourne, M. (1995), 'The intralaminar thalamic nucleii', Consciousness and Cognition, 4.

Kjaer, Troels, Camilla Bertelsen, Paola Piccini, David Brooks, Jorgen Alving, and Hans Lou. "Increased Dopamine Tone during Meditation- Induced Change of Consciousness." Cognitive Brain Research 13, no. 2 (April 2002)

Kölmel HW. 1985. Complex visual hallucinations in the hemianopic field. J Neurol Neurosurg Psychiatry.

Koenig, Harold. "Research on Religion, Spirituality, and Mental Health: A Review." Canadian Journal of Psychiatry 54, no. 5 (May 2009)

Koenig, Harold, ed. Handbook of Religion and Mental Health. San Diego, CA: Academic Press, 1998

Kraepelin E. Psychiatry: A Textbook for Students and Physicians. New York, NY: Science History Publications; 1990.

Lauglin, Charles, John McManus, and Eugene d'Aquili. Brain, Symbol, and Experience. 2nd ed. New York: Columbia University Press, 1992

Lakoff, G. and M. Johnson (1999). Philosophy in the flesh. Basic Books: New York.

LeDoux, J. E. (1996). The emotional brain. New York: Simon & Schuster.

LeDoux, J.E. (1992), 'Emotion and the amygdala', in The Amygdala:

Neurobiological Aspects of Emo- tion, Memory and Mental Dysfunction, ed J.P. Aggleton (New York: Wiley-Liss).

Levin, D.T. and Simons, D.J. (1997) Failure to detect changes to attended objects in motion pictures. Psychonomic Bulletin and Review 4, 501-6.

Levine,J. (1983) Materialism and qualia: the explanatory gap. Pacific Philosophical Quarterly 64, 354-61.

Levine,J. (2001) Purple Haze: The Puzzle of Consciousness. New York, Oxford University Press. Levine, S. (1979) A Gradual Awakening. New York, Doubleday.

Levinson, B.W. (1965) States of awareness during general anaesthesia. British Journal of Anaesthesia 37, 544-6.

Lewicki, P., Czyzewska, M. and Hoffman, H. (1987) Unconscious acquisition of complex procedural knowledge. Journal of Experimental Psychology: Learning, Memory and Cognition 13, 523-30.

Lewicki, P., Hill, T. and Bizot, E. (1988) Acquisition of procedural knowledge about a pattern of stimuli that cannot be articulated. Cognitive Psychology 20, 24-37.

Lewicki, P., Hill, T. and Czyzewska, M. (1992) Nonconscious acquisition of information. American Psychologist 47, 796-801.

Manthey S, Schubotz RI, von Cramon DY (2003). Premotor cortex in observing erroneous action: an fMRI study. Brain Res Cogn Brain Res 15: 296–307.

Mesulam MM, Mufson EJ (1982) Insula of the old world monkey. III: Efferent cortical output and comments on function. J Comp Neurol 212: 38–52.

Naskar, Abhijit. "Homo: A Brief History of Consciousness", 2015

Naskar, Abhijit. "What is Mind?", 2016

Naskar, Abhijit. "In Search of Divinity: Journey to The Kingdom of Conscience", 2016

Naskar, Abhijit. "Love, God & Neurons: Memoir of A Scientist who found himself by getting lost", 2016

Naskar, Abhijit. "Neurons of Jesus: Mind of A Teacher, Spouse & Thinker", 2017

Naskar, Abhijit. "Principia Humanitas", 2017

Naskar, Abhijit. "We Are All Black: A Treatise on Racism", 2017

Naskar, Abhijit. "Wise Mating: A Treatise on Monogamy", 2017

Naskar, Abhijit. "Illusion of Religion: A Treatise on Religious Fundamentalism", 2017

Naskar, Abhijit. "I Am The Thread: My Mission", 2017

Naskar, Abhijit. "Morality Absolute", 2017

Naskar, Abhijit. "Fabric of Humanity", 2018

Naskar, Abhijit. "The Constitution of The United Peoples of Earth", 2019

Naskar, Abhijit. "Neurons Giveth, Neurons Taketh Away | Abhijit Naskar | TEDxIIMRanchi", 2019 https://www.youtube.com/watch?v=B NX-Q0ySm80

Naskar, Abhijit. "Mission Reality", 2019

Newberg, Andrew, and Jeremy Iversen. "The Neural Basis of the Complex Mental Task of Meditation: Neurotransmitter and Neurochemical Considerations." Medical Hypotheses 61, no. 2 (2003).

Newberg, Andrew. "How God Changes Your Brain: An Introduction to Jewish Neurotheology", CCAR

Journal: The Reform Jewish Quarterly, Winter 2016.

Newberg, Andrew, and Stephanie Newberg. "A Neuropsychological Perspective on Spiritual Development." In Handbook of Spiritual Development in Childhood and Adolescence, edited by Eugene Roehlkepartain, Pamela King, Linda Wagener, and Peter Benson. London: Sage Publications, Inc., 2005

Newberg, Andrew. "The Neurotheology Link An Intersection Between Spirituality and Health", Alternative and Complimentary Therapies, Vol 21 No 1, February 2015.

Newberg, Andrew, Nancy Wintering, Dharma Khalsa, Hannah Roggenkamp, and Mark Waldman. "Meditation Effects on Cognitive Function and Cerebral Blood Flow in Subjects with Memory Loss: A Preliminary Study." Journal of Alzheimer's Disease 20, no. 2 (2010)

Nash, M. (1995), 'Glimpses of the mind', Time.

Nesse RM. Proximate and evolutionary studies of anxiety, stress and depression: synergy at the interface. Neurosci Biobehav Rev. 1999;23:895-903.

Nicolelis, Miguel. (2011) "Beyond Boundaries: The New Neuroscience of Connecting Brains with Machines---and How It Will Change Our Lives", Times Books

O'Hara, K. and Scutt, T. (1996) There is no hard problem of consciousness. Journal of Consciousness Studies 3(4), 290-302, reprinted in J. Shear (ed.) (1997) Explaining Consciousness. Cambridge, MA, MIT Press, 69-82.

O'Regan, J.K. (1992) Solving the "real" mysteries of visual perception: the world as an outside memory. Canadian Journal of Psychology 46, 461-88.

O'Regan, J.K. and Noe, A. (2001) A sensorimotor account of vision and visual consciousness. Behavioral and Brain Sciences 24(5), 883-917.

O'Regan, J.K., Rensink, R.A. and Clark,].]. (1999) Change-blindness as a result of "mudsplashes." Nature 398, 34.

Ornstein, R.E. (1977) The Psychology of Consciousness (2nd edn). New York, Harcourt.

Ornstein, R.E. (1986) The Psychology of Consciousness (3rd edn). New York, Pehguin.

Ornstein, R.E. (1992) The Evolution of Consciousness. New York, Touchstone.

Penfield W, Faulk ME (1955) The insula: further observations on its function. Brain 78: 445– 470.

Penrose, R. (1994), Shadows of the Mind (Oxford: Oxford University Press).

Penrose, R. (1989), The Emperor's New Mind: Concerning Computers, Minds and The Laws of Physics (Oxford: Oxford University Press).

Persinger, "'I would kill in God's name' role of sex, weekly church attendance, report of a religious experience and limbic lability" Perceptual and Motor Skills 1997.

Persinger "Experimental simulation of the God experience" Neurotheology 2003.

Persinger, M. A. (1993b). Personality changes following brain injury as a grief response to the loss of sense of self: Phenomenological themes as indices of local lability and neurocognitive restructuring as psycho- therapy. Psychological Reports, 72

Persinger, Corradini, Clement, Keaney, et al "Neurotheology and its convergence with neuroquantology" NeuroQuantology 2010.

Persinger, Koren and St-Pierre "The electromagnetic induction of mystical and altered states within the laboratory" Journal of Consciousness Exploration and Research 2010.

Persinger "Case report: A prototypical spontaneous 'sensed presence' of a sentient being and concomitant electroencephalographic activity in the clinical laboratory" Neurocase 2008.

Persinger and Saroka "Potential production of Hughlings Jackson's "parasitic consciousness" by physiologically-patterned weak transcerebral magnetic fields: QEEG and source localization" Epilepsy & Behavior 28 (2013).

Persinger. "The neuropsychiatry of paranormal experiences". J Neuropsychiatry Clin Neurosci 2001.

Persinger. "Neuropsychological bases of god beliefs", New York: Praeger, 1987

Persinger. "Temporal lobe epileptic signs and correlative behaviors displayed by normal populations", Journal of General Psychology, 1986

Perry BD, Pollard R. Homeostasis, stress, trauma, and adaptation. A neurodevelopmental view of childhood trauma. Child Adolesc Psychiatr Clin N Am. 1998;7:33.

Paré, D. & Llinás, R. (1995), 'Conscious and preconscious processes as seen from the standpoint of sleep-waking cycle neurophysiology', Neuropsychologia, 33.

P. S. de Laplace. Essai Philosophique sur les Probabilites [1814], in Academy des Sciences, Oeuvres Complotes de

Laplace, Vol. 7, Gauthier-Villars, Paris (1886).

Perrett DI, Harries MH, Bevan R, Thomas S, Benson PJ, Mistlin AJ, Chitty AJ, Hietanen JK, Ortega JE (1989) Frameworks of analysis for the neural representation of animate objects and actions. J Exp Bio 146: 87–113.

Phillips ML, Young AW, Senior C, Brammer M, Andrew C, Calder AJ, Bullmore ET, Perrett DI, Rowland D, Williams SC, Gray JA, David AS (1997) A specific neural substrate for perceiving facial expressions of disgust. Nature 389: 495–498.

Phillips ML, Young AW, Scott SK, Calder AJ, Andrew C, Giampietro V, Williams SC, Bullmore ET, Brammer M, Gray JA (1998) Neural responses to facial and vocal expressions of fear and disgust. Proc R Soc Lond B Biol Sci 265: 1809–1817.

Puce A, Perrett D (2003) Electrophysiological and brain imaging of biological motion. Philosoph Trans Royal Soc Lond, Series B, 358: 435–445.

Ramachandran VS. Behavioral and magnetoencephalographic correlates of plasticity in the adult human brain. Proc Natl Acad Sci USA 1993; 90: 10413–20.

Ramachandran VS. Phantom limbs, neglect syndromes, repressed memories, and Freudian psychology. Int Rev Neurobiol 1994; 37: 291–333.

Ramachandran VS. Plasticity and functional recovery in neurology. Clin Med 2005; 5: 368–73.

Ramachandran VS, Hirstein W. The perception of phantom limbs. The D. O. Hebb lecture. Brain 1998; 121: 1603–30.

Ramachandran VS, Rogers-Ramachandran D, Cobb S. Touching

the phantom limb. Nature 1995; 377: 489–90.

Ramachandran VS, Rogers-Ramachandran D. Phantom limbs and neural plasticity. Arch Neurol 2000; 57: 317–20.

Ramachandran VS, Rogers-Ramachandran D. It's all done with mirrors. Sci Am Mind 2007; 18: 16–9.

Ramachandran VS, Rogers-Ramachandran D. Sensations referred to a patient's phantom arm from another subjects intact arm: perceptual correlates of mirror neurons. Med Hypotheses 2008; 70: 1233–4.

Ramachandran VS, Rogers-Ramachandran D, Stewart M. Perceptual correlates of massive cortical reorganization. Science 1992; 258: 1159–60.

Rizzolatti G, Craighero L (2004) The mirror-neuron system. Annu Rev Neurosci 27: 169–192.

Rizzolatti G, Fogassi L, Gallese V (2001) Neurophysiological mechanisms underlying the understanding and imitation of action. Nature Rev Neurosci 2:661–670.

Rock I, Victor J. Vision and touch: an experimentally created conflict between the two senses. Science 1964; 143: 594–6.

Rose'n B, Lundborg G. Training with a mirror in rehabilitation of the hand. Scand J Plast Reconstr Surg Hand Surg 2005; 39: 104–8.

Royet JP, Plailly J, Delon-Martin C, Kareken DA, Segebarth C (2003) fMRI of emotional responses to odors: influence of hedonic valence and judgment, handedness, and gender. Neuroimage 20: 713–728.

Rozin R Haidt J and McCauley CR (2000) Disgust. In: Lewis M, Haviland-Jones JM (eds) Handbook of Emotion.

2nd Edition. Guilford Press, New York, pp 637–653.

Saxe R, Carey S, Kanwisher N (2004) Understanding other minds: linking developmental psychology and functional neuroimaging. Annu Rev Psychol 55: 87–124.

S. J. Russell and P. Norvig, Artificial intelligence: a modern approach (3rd edition): Prentice Hall, 2009.

Schienle A, Stark R, Walter B, Blecker C, Ott U, Kirsch P, Sammer G, Vaitl D (2002) The insula is not specifically involved in disgust processing: an fMRI study. Neuroreport 13: 2023–2026.

Showers MJC, Lauer EW (1961) Somatovisceral motor patterns in the insula. J Comp Neurol 117: 107–115.

Singer T, Seymour B, O'Doherty J, Kaube H, Dolan RJ, Frith CD (2004) Empathy for pain involves the affective but not the sensory components of pain. Science 303: 1157–1162.

Smith A (1759) The theory of moral sentiments (ed. 1976). Clarendon Press, Oxford.

S. N. Bose (1924). "Plancks Gesetz und Lichtquantenhypothese". Zeitschrift für Physik. 26 (1): 178–181.

Sprengelmeyer R, Rausch M, Eysel UT, Przuntek H (1998) Neural structures associated with recognition of facial expressions of basic emotions Proc R Soc Lond B Biol Sci 265: 1927–1931.

Strafella AP, Paus T (2000) Modulation of cortical excitability during action observation: a transcranial magnetic stimulation study. NeuroReport 11: 2289–2292.

Simonsen R (2015) Eating for the future: veganism and the challenge of in vitro meat. In: Stapleton P, Byers A (Hg). Biopolitics and utopia. Palgrave

Macmillan, New York (2015), S 167–190

Tanaka K (1996) Inferotemporal cortex and object vision. Ann Rev Neurosci. 19: 109–140.

Tesla N. "My Inventions", 1919

T. R. Society, "Machine learning: the power and promise of computers that learn by example," ed. The Royal Society, 2017.

Tomasello M, Call J (1997) Primate cognition. Oxford University Press, Oxford.

Tremblay C, Robert M, Pascual-Leone A, Lepore F, Nguyen DK, Carmant L, Bouthillier A, Theoret H (2004) Action observation and execution: intracranial recordings in a human subject. Neurology. 63: 937–938.

Umilta MA, Kohler E, Gallese V, Fogassi L, Fadiga L, Keysers C, Rizzolatti G (2001) "I know what you are doing": a neurophysiological study. Neuron 32: 91–101.

Von Wright G.H., (1963), Norm and Action. A Logical Inquiry, Routledge & Kegan Paul, London.

Von Wright G.H., (1976), "Determinism and the Study of Man", in Essays on Explanation and Understanding, ed. by J. Manninen and R. Tuomela, Reidel, Dordrecht.

Von Wright G.H., (1977), "What is Humanism?", The Lindlay Lecture, University of Arkansas, Lawrence, Kansas.

Von Wright G.H., (1979), "Humanism and the Humanities", in Philosophy and Grammar, ed. by S. Kanger and S. Öhman, Reidel, Dordrecht, pp. 1-16. Reprinted in von Wright (1993).

Von Wright G.H., (1980), Freedom and Determination, North-Holland Publishing Co., Amsterdam.

Von Wright G.H., (1985), Of Human Freedom, The Tanner Lectures on Human Values,

Vol. VI, ed. by S. M. McMurrin, University of Utah Press, Salt Lake City, pp. 107-70. Reprinted in von Wright (1998).

Von Wright G.H., (1993), The Tree of Knowledge and Other Essays, Brill, Leiden.

Von Wright G.H., (1997), "Progress: Fact and Fiction", in The Idea of Progress, ed. by A. Burgen et al., W. de Gruyter, Berlin, pp. 1-18.

Von Wright G.H., (1998), In the Shadow of Descartes: Essays in the Philosophy of Mind, Kluwer, Dordrecht.